Dear Luna Wilde...

A mother's journey to self-discovery, spiritual awakenings, and a sh*t ton of healing.

Leena Lemos

Cover Designed by Leena Lemos

For information regarding bulk purchases or speaking en-
gagements, please visit www.LeenaLemos.com.

ISBN: 9780578746142

Published by Leena Lemos

Printed in the United States of America

To my moon girl. Thank you for choosing me.

Preface

I was never one of those women who knew she wanted to be a mom. Perhaps it was the deep-rooted shame surrounding my sexuality or the media's depictions of mothers that made me quickly declare this journey wasn't for me.

As my peers became parents, I watched their narratives take a drastic shift towards "Just wait 'til…," as if it was a badge of honor for the suffering they endured and I would soon discover myself.

I didn't want any of that.

I told my husband that when I stopped having dreams that I was pregnant and mortified, I would know I was ready to start a family.

Those dreams never stopped.

So instead, I decided to tune them out in hopes that motherhood would make it all go away.

That didn't work either.

When my husband and I decided to start a family, my Grandma passed away.

Her death ignited a deep questioning within me. One that I'm still trying to answer to this day, but surely changed the trajectory of my life forever. And it all started with a letter:

April 13, 2018

Dear Baby,

We buried my grandma Theresa today. Her passing has ignited a fire within me, calling me to step up and accept my true calling.

I wasn't the granddaughter who knew her the best or tried the hardest. I lived five hours away and only saw her a few times a year (if I was lucky).

Throughout the three days I spent with the women of my family planning her funeral, there was a voice whispering inside of me...

"Step up," it said.

And so I did. I volunteered to give the eulogy when no one else thought they could. I knew it had to be me. All I could think to myself was, "If I truly want to be a parent, how can I not have courage when my family needs strength?"

While I had been looking forward to a few days of bereavement away from work to take a break from writing, I welcomed the opportunity to use my gift for my family. It didn't take long before the words flowed out of me into the perfect eulogy.

One thing you'll come to realize about me is that I'm fairly confident I was a vaudeville performer in a past life. The thrill of performing ignites me at my core. Yet, years of adolescent bullying and emotionally abusive relationships turned my vivacious thirst to please a crowd into a more introverted and cautious sense of self. I can't even quantify the number of times in the last decade after a presentation or performance I've thought, "I know I could have done better."

Dressed in Grandma's pearls and my Grandpa's commemorative pin for thirty years in the Postal Service, I stood up and delivered her eulogy just as I practiced. It was full of heart, humor, and Yankee references. I hit every beat. My jokes were extremely well received. It was my first moment in years maybe decades, where I felt truly proud of myself. And it was within that moment, that my courage to be all that I am was restored.

I stepped up and stepped into Me.

Now, I am fearless in the pursuit of cultivating a life that exudes kindness and enlightenment. While we wait for you, I will plant the foundation for your home. I promise to be present in each moment. To cherish you. To protect you. To teach you how to be respectful of our planet and all living things. To teach you that you are worthy. You are abundant. You are love.

I promise to find balance and grounding. I promise to let go of all that does not serve me, for my emotional baggage does not define you.

I promise to lead with love and surrender to the power of the universe to be in tune with the light I know I'm meant to put forth.

This letter is my commitment to this journey. I am mindfully nesting for your arrival.

In death there is life, and my child, I know she is now watching over you until you decide it's time to join us Earthside.

I hope there's no such thing as second-hand smoke, wherever you are. Theresa sure did love her cigarettes.

I can't wait to meet you.

With love and gratitude as deep as the universe,
Your Future Mama

P.S. You have a dog brother who's an attention whore. We'll work on that, too.

Before I wrote that letter, I was living small. I was lost. I was unhappy and I couldn't quite determine why. I was convinced that my life was only about finding mediocrity and the innate calls towards something bigger were just a funny joke.

I carried deep wounds from being bullied in high school, barely making it out of an emotionally and physically abusive relationship, and being abandoned over and over again by friends and significant others I thought were the ones.

I didn't know who I was anymore, but that letter was my commitment to finding her again. If I've learned anything since that April, it's this:

The journey to healing, self-love, and finding the light within is just a series of letters to ourselves. These "letters" are small commitments that we make when we can't imagine going any further with our present circumstances. They are small pivots in the right direction to discovering our true power. They are slivers of our hearts that we vulnerably surrender to the universe.

I started writing these letters to my daughter as a way to express what was on my heart when I thought no one else would listen. They are my safe space to heal, question the system, release deep wounds, and come back home to myself.

As I cultivated more courage and began sharing my stories with the world through my company, House of Enlightenedhood, I realized the universality of our experiences. So many other mothers resonated with what I thought I was dealing with all by myself.

It is now my mission to share the raw and multi-faceted experience that is motherhood and womanhood, because I know you need to hear it, too. I hope this book will give you the permission you're waiting for (although, you don't need it from me!) to be all that you are and honor your story, whether or not it looks anything like mine.

I believe letters are the most honest way to communicate because they travel in a direct line from heart to hand to paper.

This book is my heart song for any mother who is ready to lead with light and own the depths of the responsibility she's been given.

And while I do not intend for Luna Wilde to read these letters anytime soon, I hope the world she exists in as a woman and a mother (if that's the path she chooses) looks a lot different from the one that existed when they were written.

I know in the deepest corners of my soul it will be.

A Letter About Guacamole

Dear Luna Wilde,

I wrote him a letter after our first date (I guess it's just something I do).

> **March 1, 2013**
> *If you're reading this, it means we're about to get married. I'm just writing this now to tell you that from the second I saw you, I knew you were the one. And, from the second I heard your voice, I knew I couldn't spend another day without it. I love you.*

Perhaps it was our shared fondness for chunky guacamole or the fact that I spent the entire night with my winter coat around my waist, the zipper holding my carefully-selected red blouse hostage inside (talk about a mortifying first date)...I just knew.

It had been five months since I moved to New Jersey to pursue my master's degree and what I thought was the happy ending to a four-year rollercoaster of a relationship.

Two weeks after moving to an entirely new state where I had zero roots, I was dumped. I may or may not have told him I hoped Hurricane Sandy would blow him away, but enough about him.

On Valentine's Day, Breanne, a friend from my graduate program, insisted I meet her friend from high school and gave me his name.

That night, I went home and did what any good Millennial would do—I put on my sleuthing pants and internet stalked the shit out of him.

Two weeks and some casual texting later, we went on a first date with Breanne and her boyfriend on the Upper West Side of Manhattan. He paid for dinner and drinks, kindly paid no attention to my rogue zipper, let me talk about myself all night, and even drove me home.

Forty-eight hours later, he took me on our second date. We went to Target, had guacamole at his go-to local Mexican restaurant, and drooled over a playpen full of puppies. Then, he took me home to meet his entire Colombian family. As I'm writing this, I realize it seems fast for a second date, but it wasn't.

2

Not soon after, we found ourselves on a stay-cation in New York City. We frolicked around Central Park, joked about Skunk Monkeys as a good band name at the Natural History Museum, made a "what-if-we-get-separated-on-the-subway" plan, and took my maiden pedestrian voyage across the Brooklyn Bridge.

It was a warm March day. The sun glistened behind him as he watched me soak it all in. The stoic Manhattan skyline. The urgency of the bells from the local bicyclists trying to avoid the dilly-dallying, selfie-stick-obsessed tourists. The smell of a chilled New York air awakening to spring.

The boy on the Brooklyn Bridge grabbed my hand, almost to feel it all again for the first time. That night, he asked me to be his girlfriend at Salvation Taco in between a few highly-competitive ping pong games. I still have the coaster from the drink I nursed while he sweetly mumbled through asking.

———————————

The boy on the Brooklyn Bridge has made loving someone so effortless. He is kind, patient, and extremely silly. He lets me dance to the beat of my own drum and follows quietly behind, always having my back.

Your Aunt Chloe read the letter I wrote after our first date during her speech at our wedding. Everyone cried. Soon after, a pop-up thunderstorm rolled in and left behind a double rainbow. It was extraordinary. In that moment, I was Dorothy, discovering the truth about what's over the rainbow.

It was home.

The boy on the Brooklyn Bridge is my husband and he is my home. He has always made me feel safe and loved.
When that boy found out he was going to be a father, we cried and prayed our future child would like guacamole.

Turns out you do.

With love and gratitude as deep as the universe,
Your Mama

A Letter About Pregnancy Cravings

Dear Luna Wilde,

I wish I had a dollar for every time someone asked me what I am craving while pregnant with you.

Not only am I annoyed, but I would be annoyed AND rich.

During this pregnancy, I am starting to question the shallow rhetoric our society created around pregnant women.

That, "How are you?" people merely ask to acknowledge you're in the same room (but don't really care about the answer), has shifted to, "What are your pregnancy cravings?"

Why do everyone and their mom need to know what I am eating? Why don't they want to discuss the LITERAL miracle of life inside of me?

Are they genuinely curious about what I am shoveling into my mouth or are they just too scared to reach beyond these useless yet common colloquialisms?

My soul is being cracked open in the biggest transformation of my life and absolutely no one is acknowledging it.

Why is no one asking me if I have dreamed of you? (Yerp.)

If I have seen your face? (I have, thanks for asking.)

If I am worried that my emotional baggage can transfer through the umbilical cord? (Absolutely fucking worried.)

What I imagine this next life chapter will be like? (Y'all keep telling me it's terrible.)

How I will feel watching my husband look at our little girl with so much love in his eyes? (Like my heart will literally explode, duh.)

Fuck cravings. My soul needs a different kind of food. And you are my soul food sherpa. (That sounded more eloquent in my head.)

When our society downsizes pregnancy to cravings, hormonal outbursts, and beach ball vibes, we create a shallow container for its immense beauty and deeply spiritual and transformative properties to exist.

This limits the space for vulnerable and authentic conversations about what it means to become a mother as our bodies and soul transform through the sacred creation of life.

We've cut off the lifeline to support services because we're too afraid to admit that our experience isn't what we've been told it should be.

Thank you for leading me to question and shift the conversation. Because of you, my soul food sherpa, I am finding the courage to speak up about weird cultural constructs we've created and shine light in a new direction.

Because of you, I realized that so many women feel the same, but didn't have the courage to speak out against the way it's always been done. It's time for a new way. That's why you've decided to come Earthside, isn't it?

And I am craving pickles and dark chocolate almond milk, in case you were wondering.

With love and gratitude as deep as the universe,
Your Mama

A Letter About The American Dream

Dear Luna Wilde,

I've been "spiritual" as long as I can remember but I didn't give myself that label until my later twenties. There's always been a part of me that I have never been able to put my finger on.

A part of me that was suppressed.
A part of me that was different than everyone else.
A part of me that was made for something larger than myself.

For most of my life, that longing for more caused a great deal of anguish. We're bred into this modern world without critical thinking skills and the ability to see beyond the tunnel vision carefully laid out before us.

Anything that isn't in alignment with science or medicine is deemed crazy, conspiracy, or woo woo. I'm realizing that "crazy" is an often-used label for patriarchy-based suppression.

Women fully owning their power with an understanding of how the universe works? They crazy. Let's burn 'em.

A woman who was Christ's equal and preached that true ascension was a self-led journey to the highest good within your heart? She crazy. Let's bury her gospel and call her a prostitute.

Women calling out men for being abusive and greedy pigs? They crazy. Let's not believe them and make them look like fools.

I digress. This isn't a rant about how the patriarchy has suppressed our power (or is it?).

I've always known there is so much more to life than meets the eye but was never given firm confirmation by anyone or anything.

Now, as I've discovered, we are spiritual beings. Some of us will remember in this lifetime. Some of us won't.

To me, spirituality is not about the woo woo, but instead, discovering the parts of myself that were left out of the narrative.

The narrative that pre-generated each chapter of my life:

Be a good girl, get good grades, participate in resume-worthy extracurriculars, get into a good college, earn a degree, get a good job, marry my soulmate, buy a house with a white picket fence, pop out some babies, have a group of frenemies to drink wine with and complain about our spouses and children, become a slave to my child's extracurriculars, and wash, rinse, and repeat until my children are secured to the same conveyor belt.

All for what? To feel like a failure when I can't afford the fence, let alone the house, because of my crippling student loan debt? To feel unfulfilled when only a fraction of my potential is considered in the workforce? To feel alone when I can't seem to belong to a friend group? To feel shame about my womanhood? There has to be more to life, right?

There is, and this deep ache for something more, my spirituality, is what saved me from extreme self-doubt.

There's part of me that *is* suppressed and I'm working hard to excavate it. A part that is full of wisdom, insight, and confidence in her physical and energetic body. A part that wasn't taught she has the capability to heal herself, influence the energies of the universe, and find the answers within.

There's a part of me that *is* different than everyone else. And that's what makes the world so beautiful. We are all here to learn different lessons on unique paths. Conformity is over-rated. Authenticity is the key to uncovering our true selves.

There's a part of me that *is* made for something larger than myself. There is more to life than labels, careers, money, and all of the things we think we need to be happy and success-ful. In the grand scheme of the universe, they are irrelevant (although I'm still trying to convince myself of this, ugh).

So, if being spiritual is really just a journey to our best selves in the highest good of this human experience, why is there so much stigma? So much doubt? So much fear? So much misinformation?

That's what I'm determined to uncover. I'll report back soon.

With love and gratitude as deep as the universe,
Your Mama

A Letter About White Flags

Dear Luna Wilde,

In 2012, I moved to New Jersey for the boy I thought I was going to marry. The move was the pinnacle to an on-again-off-again love story that I thought was going to have a fairy-tale ending (that's what the movies teach us, right?).

I don't want to dwell too much on the past, but our story went a little like this:

Boy and girl meet first day of college. Boy and girl fall recklessly in love. Boy helps to heal girl's wounds. Boy and girl are inseparable. Boy tells girl he wants to marry her on New Year's Eve. Boy breaks up with girl three days later while she's staying at his house over winter break, six hours away from home. Boy and girl go their separate ways and transfer schools. Boy and girl spend three years apart living their own lives. Boy sends girl message before their senior year of college to confess he's never stopped loving her. Boy and girl get back together but have a long distance relationship. Girl decides to attend graduate school near boy to finally be together once and for all. Boy and girl move in together. Boy breaks up with girl (again) two weeks later. Boy and girl still live together. Girl sleeps on air mattress in the living room. Girl tells boy she wishes he would blow away in the wind. Hurricane Sandy knocks out all the electricity for days. Boy moves out a few weeks later.

I distinctly remember thinking as we unpacked our boxes how grateful I was that we would never have to worry about which items belonged to whom ever again. Little did I know, we would be arguing over *It's Always Sunny in Philadelphia* DVDs a few weeks later.

He couldn't even look at me when he told me he didn't love me anymore. He asked me to move all the things out of our bedroom. I lived in the corner of the living room surrounded by my things for weeks before I dared to reach out to my parents and admit defeat.

They drove down to New Jersey to take me home and help me heal. I spent a week in my childhood bedroom, curled up in a deflated ball, hoping I'd wake up from my worst nightmare.

Just when I thought I had finally found my way, just when I thought I had made it to Oz, life had different plans.

It came time to make a decision. Would I wave my white flag in defeat, move back home, and start over? Or would I stay in New Jersey and find the strength to piece back together a broken life without any roots?

"Psssssst," the whisper said. "Don't wave your white flag."

And while I may not have heard it as clearly, I did have a distinct feeling in my heart that I had to stay in New Jersey.

I didn't know why, but I knew in that moment that no matter what, I had the strength to see it through.

And so I did. And it is what led me to you.

With love and gratitude as deep as the universe,
Your Mama

A Letter About Lessons

Dear Luna Wilde,

Here's a list of things I hope to teach you in this lifetime:

1. To honor all living things
2. To treat Mother Earth with respect
3. To see your body as a sacred temple
4. To learn the difference between your and you're
5. To find beauty in the seemingly mundane
6. To follow your heart
7. To value experiences over material things
8. To interact with others with love and dignity
9. To discover the magic in vulnerability
10. To chew with your mouth closed
11. To appreciate nature over technology

Let's check back in twenty years and see how I did.

With love and gratitude as deep as the universe,
Your Mama

A Letter About Pitocin

Dear Luna Wilde,

I feel so much shame around my birth experience.

It wasn't miraculous. It wasn't the happiest moment of my life. It wasn't profound like I imagined.

I wasn't strong. I wasn't empowered. I don't feel proud of my body for what it accomplished as it brought you to us.

As my birth canal (have I ever written those words before?) continued to (unnaturally) prepare for you, I sucked on pieces of ice as your Dad read me excerpts from Chip Gains's new book.

I floated in and out of consciousness and on and off an oxygen mask as your heart rate fluctuated with my contractions.

When it was time, your Dad was by my side.

My doctor took several phone calls as I pushed.

Only one wonderful nurse was with us for the entire journey. I wish I could remember her name to thank her.

It took an hour and thirty-one minutes of active labor and an hour and twenty of that was spent trying to get your head unstuck from my pelvic bone.

As soon as you finally arrived, you were whisked away by residents and NICU nurses, because you swallowed your meconium.

There was no immediate placement of you on my chest. I barely caught a glimpse of your face.

Your Dad anxiously paced as they vacuumed your airways and cleaned you up.

When you finally received a clean bill of health, we were only able to spend a few moments together as a family before they took you to the nursery.

As I wait for your return, I feel sorrow that I am so numb. I don't know if it's the adrenaline, the shock, or the medication in my system.

I hope you'll forgive me.

I feel so heartbroken that we haven't gotten to know each other yet.

Oh, how I am dying to know you.

With love and gratitude as deep as the universe,
Your Mama

A Letter About Awareness

Dear Luna Wilde,

As we left the hospital, a nurse in the elevator commented that she's never seen a newborn so awake and aware.

You've been Earthside for less than forty-eight hours and people are already in awe of your presence.

I already know I'm in for a lifetime of awe just because you... are you.

With love and gratitude as deep as the universe,
Your Mama

A Letter About Efficiency

Dear Luna Wilde,

Why is our worth as mothers determined by our baby's eating and sleeping habits?

Call me petty, but I did some "quantitative research" before writing you this letter.

In the last month of your life...

> The number of times I've been asked if you sleep and eat well: 147

> The number of times I've been asked if I am well: 2 (both by my Mom)

Is this really what it's like to transition into motherhood? What happened to the "it takes a village" bullshit?

Why aren't the women I know, who have been through this, more concerned about my wellbeing?

Why has no one offered any help?

Why do I feel like such a tarnished pile of stretched out organs and bones?

This idea of efficiency with a newborn just screams "patriarchy!" and "Industrial Revolution!" to me. Did you know that our society didn't value sleeping continuously through the night until we were required to work outside of the home?

Most adults still don't sleep all the way through the night. You've been trying for one month. I'd say your snoozing habits are completely appropriate for your age.

But why is it still the only thing we can seem to ask new moms?

Why have we, as a society, taken their power away?

These are the things that keep me up at night (other than you).

With love and gratitude as deep as the universe,
Your Mama

A Letter About Missions

Dear Luna Wilde,

Something is happening within me. Something I can only describe as a true spiritual awakening.

I feel like I'm on the verge of a huge metamorphosis. Oh, how I desperately want to be done with this current version of me. There is so much more I'm ready to share with the world.

In my third trimester, a word, that I believe was a Divine download, came to me. Enlightenedhood.

I know I have to follow where it leads.

So, since your arrival, I've been laying the stones for this idea of Enlightenedhood to become a safe container for spiritual women who want to lead with light and intention while digging into the depths of their own soul.

I truly think there is something there that has yet to be discussed.

Something life changing. Something world changing.

I think I've finally found what I came to this Earth to do. And while I'm still not exactly sure what Enlightenedhood will become, I do know I will follow my intuition and trust that this is my path.

I promise I won't let you down.

With love and gratitude as deep as the universe,
Your Mama

A Letter About Gerald

Dear Luna Wilde,

I want to tell you about Gerald.

Gerald fell in love with Theresa at age fifteen. He married her three years later. He sold his plane to buy their first house. He loved clocks, guns, trains, cigarettes, writing letters, and Theresa's chocolate cake. He raised three children and supported them with over thirty years of dedication to the Postal Service. He was a professional bullshitter, infamous prankster, and the life of the party. His household of chiming clocks slowly became dissonant as he withered away.

Theresa's name was the last thing the Alzheimer's took.

Gerald is my mother's father. And he became my spirit guide the day he died.

When Gerald passed, I was on the verge of failing out of the tenth grade because of low attendance. I was bullied, lost my athletic outlet due to an undiagnosable injury, and was in a manipulative and abusive relationship that started it all.

As a freshman, I felt on top of the world. I was a master of elite choirs and cabaret performances, rising to a promising mid-distance track career, and had one of the highest GPAs in my class.

The summer before tenth grade, I was in the midst of rekindling a romance with a middle school boyfriend when I met my best friend's cousin, Mr. Pennsylvania. He was charming, goofy, and exotic compared to the fifty-something boys I had known since kindergarten.

When I chose Mr. Pennsylvania over Mr. Middle School, I never imagined the repercussions from one seemingly summer fling.

Feeling rejected and hurt, Mr. Middle School rebelled, turning my friends against me and the classroom and online space into a war zone.

Members who were part of my hate club proudly stated it in their instant messaging profiles (old person talk for bios) and made a conscious and daily effort to send me anonymous messages calling me a whore and asking me to stop showing up to school.

And so I did. I poured all of my attention into a long-distance relationship with Mr. Pennsylvania, riding the wave of the honeymoon phase...until it turned abusive.

The first time he hit me was because I wrote a crooked letter on his school poster. It was out of nowhere and changed everything. The second time he threw the house phone at my head. It missed and dented the wall on impact. The third time he pushed me onto the asphalt of the P&C parking lot. The fall sprained my wrist.

On top of the violent outbursts, he was emotionally manipulative. He used my struggles at school as a way to keep me in his grasp, knowing I had nowhere else to go. In addition to the hate messages I received from my classmates, I also received daily "common courtesy" messages that Mr. Pennsylvania was cheating with a revolving door of girls from his hometown.

With storms coming at me from all angles, I began to wither. My body felt like it weighed five hundred pounds. An unexplainable stabbing pain kept manifesting in my back until I could no longer run and then I could no longer move.

I was paralyzed. I was drowning.

26

I stopped showing up to school. I was a shell. My relationship with my parents turned toxic. I didn't have the courage
to share what I was really going through and still haven't as I
write these words. Instead, I let them believe that I was a
sex-crazed rebellious teenager that didn't care. We tried to
work it out throughout the winter in counseling but it didn't
go anywhere because I was living a lie.

One day in March, I prepped the list of all the reasons I
should get picked up early from school before I called my
Dad to come get me. My Grandpa dying was first on the list.

My Dad told me the news in the high school parking lot.

His funeral was the most beautiful day. Sun glistened
through the windows illuminating the dust as we all said our
goodbyes to his open casket. Your Aunt Chloe, my cousin
Julie and I joined hands and tears as we approached him. It
was the first time I ever saw a dead body.

Gerald would be the type to pop up from the casket and
scare the shit out of us like some Candid Camera practical
joke, but we all knew he was really gone, as we had all
watched the Alzheimer's steal his sparkle away over the
years.

After he was diagnosed, yet still fairly healthy, my Dad remembers him saying that the nice thing about the disease is that, "You meet new people every day. Some strangers, and some you forgot you met the day before."

At his funeral, my Grandma Theresa did not cry. She just stood at the head of the casket and whispered sweet nothings to him in between grieving family members.

"You were quite the boy, Gerald," she muttered, "you were really something."

My heart has never accepted anything more true. Married for over fifty years with a house, a home, even in his death, my Grandpa was still that charismatic boy that she fell in love with at fifteen, and still to this day, that breaks my heart.

After he passed, Gerald became my protector during one of my lowest lows. He came to me in my dreams, giving me the strength I needed to make it through each day.

"You *do* have the strength to do it all," he would say. "You have such a beautiful life on the other side of this."

I finally gained the courage to end it with Mr. Pennsylvania during my senior year. While I regret not leaving sooner, if it wasn't for him, I wouldn't be writing these words to you.

It was at the college we planned to attend together where I met the next boy who would break my heart. He would be the one to lead me to New Jersey, where I would meet your Dad and discover my true self. But that's a story for a different day.

Gerald understood that my intuition and spirituality needed to sit on the back burner so I could fully live out certain experiences to bring me to my truth. So, he watched from afar until I was ready, and just as I was, he reunited with Theresa again.

I know in my heart that Gerald and Theresa's deaths played such a significant role in bringing you to me.

And while it feels cathartic to share all of that, I'm fairly certain you already know all of this because you've met them on the other side.

Whenever I show you pictures of them you smile as if you know exactly who they are.

You point at their gold fiftieth-anniversary clock and laugh and smile as you babble and coo at them in the corner.

Sometimes I'm simply in awe of how interconnected we truly are. I can't wait to ask you more about them.

With love and gratitude as deep as the universe,
Your Mama

A Letter About Accepting Love

Dear Luna Wilde,

I keep having these crazy dreams and waking up with an ache in my heart. It took a lot of reflection to determine why they were so gut-wrenching.

When I discovered the reason, my heart sank.

These dreams hurt so badly because I keep finding myself in situations where I feel like being a mother is a reason to accept less love. To feel less than compared to a woman who hasn't given birth.

As a society, we've become conditioned to think that being a creator of the next generation somehow tarnishes us as women.

We're not as beautiful, not as sexy, not as lovable, not as worthy, not as...you name it, after our body literally creates another human (a.k.a. you).

We are taught to feel shame, to "fix the flaws," and to con-
form to a standard that is unrealistic and un-celebratory of
the miracle of life.

And I'm fucking done with that.

Women are not broken. Women are enough. Women are
goddamn powerful.

Our time to shine is now and I'm trying to rewrite that history
to reclaim that power for you.

With love and gratitude as deep as the universe,
Your Mama

A Letter About the Spiritual Closet

Dear Luna Wilde,

I am tiptoeing out of the spiritual closet and discovered it can be extremely lonely. There's a pretentiousness that comes with spirituality and personal development that triggers others.

As I start to question, they are questioning me.

But really, it's a huge misunderstanding.

I am not spiritual because I want to be better than anyone else. I am spiritual because I am discovering the tools to help heal and empower the heart that thought she was *less than* for so many years.

And boy, do I still have a long way to go in the worthiness department.

But the real irony? Through the continuous lessons of my spiritual journey, I am able to see all people through a lens of love and understanding.

And with that, comes an ability to move beyond judgment towards others.

To me, being "spiritual" is about finding love, gratitude, connectedness, and humility in all things.

Spirituality is about coming home to yourself. I just want to know who I am. I want to be able to love myself with the same depth that I love you.

Nothing more. I wish others could see that.

Maybe someday they will.

With love and gratitude as deep as the universe,
Your Mama

A Letter About Energy

Dear Luna Wilde,

Sometimes, I catch you staring very intently at your hands, studying every inch of them.

I like to imagine you can see the pure and powerful energy coming out of them.

Oh, how powerful you are.

With love and gratitude as deep as the universe,
Your Mama

A Letter About The Ocean

Dear Luna Wilde,

Today, we took you to the ocean for the first time. New Jerseyans call it "The Shore." I refuse to call it that as part of my very important anti-Jersey girl identity.

It was the first time I sat on a New Jersey beach since moving here seven years ago. Your Dad and I went once when we first started dating, but it rained. He's convinced he's cursed with rainy beach days so we never went back (Also, bumper-to-bumper Parkway traffic just to sit on a crowded beach for a few hours? No thanks.).

The important part of this trip I want to share with you is not how frustrating the wind was as it blew our sad-excuse-for-an-umbrella every which way or how fucking cute you were in your little beach hat and flamingo bathing suit. Instead, I want to tell you about the ocean.

For years, I convinced myself I didn't need her. That I was a lake soul through and through. But about a month ago, I started to feel that what I was looking for was at the beach.

And it was a feeling that wouldn't go away. So, I told your Dad we had to go, but first I must rewind.

A few weeks ago, I went to my obstetrician because I still have a lot of pain from giving birth. At five months postpartum (ha, just kidding it's actually six weeks), we're told we should be "back to normal" and life, relationships, etc., should resume as before. I am nowhere close to that.

I've sat here thinking about how I want to share what happened during this appointment while honoring the weight of the wound it left on my heart, so here's my attempt:

What I was looking for: A concern for what might be going on, a discussion about my struggle with countless health problems postpartum, concern for my mental health, an intimate discussion of how I can begin to feel like myself again, and reassurance that this is, in fact, normal.

What I got: A quick declaration that nothing appeared wrong, an inquisition of whether or not I'm ready to have more children yet, sex positions to manage the pain, and then just when I couldn't feel any worse, as I was getting dressed, my doctor stuck her head back in the door, as if to have some lasting "impactful words" and said, "You know, you should really try exercising."

Door shut.

To say this appointment broke me is completely accurate. I sat in my car and cried for an hour in the driveway before picking you up from your Abuelita's house.

Now, back to the ocean. I told your Dad I needed a little time alone and made my way to the water in a t-shirt and shorts. I sheepishly put my toes in the water, worried that too much of my body was on full display for an entire audience of beach-goers. Sorry, shoregoers.

But then, something wonderful happened. As I waded deeper and deeper into the water, I was no longer a body, but a soul connected with the ocean.

I began to feel weightless as I floated with the ebb and flow of the waves.

I was free.

As I bobbed and escaped from the crashing waves beneath the water, not once did I think about my body and how ashamed I felt of it.

Not once did I think about how my body betrayed me with infection after infection, still holding onto 50 pounds of extra weight.

I learned an important lesson in the Atlantic. It is a reminder that we are so much more than our bodies.

It is our system that told me my body was wrong and it is me who reclaimed the power to decide it can be anything I want it to be.

The ocean helped remind me of that and now I'm here to remind you. Never forget, you are a soul who has a body.

Not the other way around.

With love and gratitude as deep as the universe,
Your Mama

A Letter About Prenatal Depression

Dear Luna Wilde,

One month and two days before you joined us Earthside, I wrote a four-word journal entry. It said:

> *I feel so lonely.*

All I could think about in the last few months of pregnancy was how every passing moment got me closer to meeting someone who finally loves me unconditionally.

I felt so unloved and so undersupported.

At the doctor's office, I felt like cattle. Herded into a room. Weighed. Measured. Insides listened to. Forced to pee in a cup.

Not once did I feel like an empowered woman about to take one of the most beautiful and natural journeys possible.

I didn't take any birthing classes and I sure as hell gave my power away to our current medical system.

But if I regret anything most from my pregnancy, it was my choice to be induced at only two days overdue so I could selfishly meet you sooner.

And I'm sorry for any trauma that it caused you, as you were brought into this world before our bodies decided we were ready. It still hurts my heart to think about it.

I thought when you were here you would make all the pain go away. And in a way, you did.

But I also learned we are the only ones who can take away our pain.

Thank you for showing me how to do that.

I'm a work in progress.

With love and gratitude as deep as the universe,
Your Mama

A Letter About September 11th

Dear Luna Wilde,

Almost twenty years ago, my world changed forever. We became vulnerable, more fearful, and unsure of normalcy.

I remember exactly where I was, in your Great-Grandmother's '98 hatchback Civic, when she told me the towers were gone.

We stood on the top floor just the year before.

Your Grandfather watched them go up, floor by floor, from his bedroom window on Water Street.

That night was the first time I ever remember using writing as a form of healing. At just eleven years old, I wrote the following words about how scared I was and how, more than ever, we needed to embrace one another and come together to prove that hatred never wins.

> ### September 11, 2001
> *I'm sure you've heard the news by now. I thought that in my lifetime there weren't going to be any wars,*

bombings, or so on. I thought the world would be mature enough and smart enough to solve the problems and not take other innocent people's lives as an answer. I thought the world was secure enough to keep my family and me safe. Now I don't know what to think.

But now...imagine peace and harmony. Now the whole world has just joined together helping one another even not knowing who they are. Everyone can help in some way. Don't you feel like you're confused deciding if this really happened? Thinking how awful it is for such to do. As I leave you, here are some wise words that John Lennon once said, "Come together."

Now as a mother, I have that same fear that you will someday know this sentiment, and perhaps see the world crash before you. All I can promise is that every day, we will face uncertainty together and I will be your rock in times of chaos.

With vulnerability comes growth and strength, and I know you will conquer the world no matter what comes your way.

With love and gratitude as deep as the universe,
Your Mama

A Letter About Showers

Dear Luna Wilde,

Sometimes I like to sit in the shower with all the lights off and pretend I am a wild goddess in a pristine hot spring, bathing under the night sky.

The pounding hot water on my chest makes me feel weightless and unaware of all the parts of my body that were unloved for so long.

If you find yourself traveling to different dimensions in the shower, it's because I opened the portal long ago.

Anyone who reads this letter might question my sanity, but I know you get it.

With love and gratitude as deep as the universe,
Your Mama

A Letter About Waves

Dear Luna Wilde,

My father's father revealed he was dying from Stage Four Lung Cancer in a casual email to us titled "Update."

———————————————

I remember clearly that it was Christmas Eve of my sophomore year of high school, a year that in thought makes me queasy. My father picked me up from my best friend's house who lived on the other side of the lake.

My Dad and I used to do quirky things together, like chase hot air balloons until they landed in a rural cornfield or flatten coins on the nearby train tracks.

That day's mission was to discover which way around the lake was faster. He already clocked one way.

On our way down the east shore of the lake towards home, the Christmas sun descended, changing its own orange face to a radiant blue.

My Dad knew I was having a hard time. To my parents, I was a stranger sulking around their house, a black hole sucking up their happiness, and a grey blob of matter buckled in the back seat of the car.

He also knew that this wasn't intentional. I didn't mean to be bullied by my own friends, I didn't mean to end my promising running career with undiagnosable back pain, and I didn't intend to melt into nothing.

"I had a hard year during tenth grade as well," he said, looking over into the orange oblivion that cascaded on the passenger side.

"You did?" I was curious to hear what he would try to compare my situation to. My Dad's good with numbers, and he's good with words in the literate sense. Emotions weren't his thing, and neither was sharing them.

He paused for a moment and harvested his words carefully before he spoke. "This day, thirty-two years ago, was the last night I spent with my Dad before he left on Christmas."

He began to cry. I could only recall him crying one other time. At Gerald's funeral.

I didn't need to hear any more to understand the depths of his pain. After my father shared that piece of his soul, I could never relate to my Grandfather the way I had before. I felt misled about who he really was and protective against the pain he caused my father.

My father's father was always called "Grandpapa." His life-style was ideal for that of a young child. He lived on the Gulf of Mexico in Sarasota, Florida, owned a Yorkie that accepted vegetables as means for going to bed, and had a stuffed toy rabbit collection, also known as the "Bun" family.

From what I know, it was my birth that sparked forgiveness in my father, allowing my Grandfather to slowly, yet distantly, be a part of my life.

Throughout my childhood, my family gathered every few years on Siesta Key for a week-long reunion. I have such fond memories of the soft white sand, the seaweed hair my Uncle sported on his balding head, and the subliminal life mantra my Grandpa taught us while playing in the crystal blue gulf water.

"No wave can knock me down," he would chant as the tide rolled in and out. We'd giggle and admire his strength as he stood fearlessly in the current, withstanding every crash and splash that the ocean threw at him.

The irony of it all? The man I saw as charismatic, strong, and fearless, was all of those things. Just not to us.

My father's father was a humanitarian. He fought hard for equality and wrote letters about things he deemed unjust. He marched on Washington in 1963 with Martin Luther King Jr. and joined civil rights activists around the country to help fight for justice. He even got locked up for it.

He was a minister-turned-atheist who's mission later in life became to empower the marginalized and lend a helping hand.

He led his life being a father to good causes, but not to his own family.

He passed today, eleven days after sending the fateful email. All three of his children found out at the airport after flying thousands of miles to rush to his bedside.

Grieving his passing feels complicated. My heart breaks for his children who didn't make it in time.

It breaks for my father's mother, who already mourned his departure decades before.

It breaks for his wife, who was the love of his life and his light for over thirty years.

Yet, despite it all, in his death there is only love.

As much as I yearned for him to show up more and accept him as a loving grandfather in my adulthood, I can't help but reflect on what his life gave me.

I can dwell on the fact that he never called me on my birthday or Christmas, that our correspondences were through emails, or that he left deep wounds on our family, but I choose gratitude.

Because of his actions on that Christmas, my father vowed to rewrite his fatherhood story and break the cycle.

As a result, I grew up with the most present, loving, thoughtful, and supportive father, who vowed to make each Christmas a special day full of quality family time and rich experiences.

Because my Grandfather welcomed us into his home, I have years of fond memories in Sarasota and Siesta Key. When we visited as kids, he took us to our usual spots: Taco Bell, Moat Marine to see the manatees, and dessert at Piggy's Old Fashioned Ice Cream. I can still taste the bubble gum flavor and smell the aging cones.

Because of his willingness to accept people for who they were, I met people from all walks of life, sexual orientations, and cultural backgrounds during my time spent with him at his churches and support groups.

Because he followed in his father's footsteps and became a minister, he was able to officiate my wedding at the Ithaca Farmer's Market. I appointed him this position as an act of love, one of very few I could truly give him.

Because of him, I am analytical, mindful, and drawn to making the world a better place.

Despite feeling grateful for all the gifts he gave me in his lifetime (even if they weren't the ones I thought I wanted), the most complicated part of his death is the guilt I carry with me.

I feel guilty I stopped responding to his emails.

I feel guilty I didn't pick up the phone and call him.

I feel guilty I didn't make more of an effort to visit.

I feel guilty that perhaps my over-analyzed version of him was skewed.

Last night before he passed, I met him under a tree in deep meditation. I apologized for not showing up. He apologized for the same.

I told him how hard it was to allow myself to fully love him because I held a grudge for his past decisions.

He told me he understood. We hugged and forgave. We gave each other grace and love.

As I watched his soul dance upward into a white light, he told me to remember "The Helpers Hope" and carry it with me beyond his death.

After my Mom called me with the news, I looked back to old emails where he had the saying in his signature. It read:

The Helpers Hope
Feel the Love.
Celebrate What You Have.
Help Where You Can.
Be at One with What Is.

With those words in your back pocket, my love, no wave will ever be able to knock you down.

With love and gratitude as deep as the universe,
Your Mama

A Letter About Fear

Dear Luna Wilde,

Remember when I wrote to you and shared that I was starting to come out of the spiritual closet?

There is nothing I want more in the world than to be freely me. To be powerful as me. To embrace all that I am.

But I cannot get past the fear. I am so scared of being judged. I am so scared of being bullied again.

Sometimes the fear consumes me to a point that I can't breathe, and I just need to tell someone.

Thank you for listening.

With love and gratitude as deep as the universe,
Your Mama

A Letter About Feminine Power

Dear Luna Wilde,

The way I grew up, young girls were fear-mongered by teenage pregnancy, and that fear is something I carried with me into my marriage.

I remember telling your Dad I knew I'd be ready for children when I stopped having dreams that I was pregnant and feeling ashamed.

Even as a grown-ass-married-woman in the prime of her child-bearing years, I still felt like I would be judged and looked down upon for getting pregnant.

I lived in this weird dichotomy, where almost none of my close friends were married or having kids, yet felt pressured from your Dad's family as the only couple without kids. I felt judged for thinking of having kids and also judged for not having them yet.

Please don't take this personally, but I was never one of those women who spent her whole life knowing her purpose was to be a mother. Perhaps it was the fact that I hadn't yet stepped into my true feminine power (okay, obviously still working on that one because writing that made me feel a little icky) or the fact that I was terrified.

I was terrified of being seen as less than from years of conditioning that pregnancy was bad. I was terrified to bring a soul like you into this world where the true worth of Mother Earth, women, animals, minorities, and so many more are not honored by our society.

I was terrified that perhaps I actually don't know as much as I assume and that I was going to set you up for failure, let you down, or fuck you up. I haven't yet, have I?

Before you were conceived and I made the decision I wanted to become a mother, I was told multiple times by intuitive advisors, palm readers, and an astrologer that my life would begin after my daughter arrived.

The first few times I heard it, I tried to ignore the profoundness of what it meant.

But then, the whispers wouldn't go away.

"Pssssst, she will bring a new version of you when she comes."

And they were right, you are the catalyst that brought me to my true self and my true path.

This is my promise to you. I will never make you feel ashamed for your body or your feminine power.

My hope is that when you are ready to read this, you will not have any similar experiences that relate.

And like I've promised in so many of my letters, I will do everything I can to make that so.

With love and gratitude as deep as the universe,
Your Mama

A Letter About Old Souls

Dear Luna Wilde,

What's it like being an old soul in a baby's body?

To sit in your own poop?

To cry as a means of communication?

Do you have access to your full consciousness or just a little nugget?

Would love to know.

With love and gratitude as deep as the universe,
Your Mama

A Letter About Postpartum Depression

Dear Luna Wilde,

For months, I convinced myself that I am kicking ass at this whole motherhood thing.

I was so energized by my mission to launch Enlightenedhood as you slept that the lows didn't feel too dire.

I'm taking care of you by day and building a global movement by night. I spend hours connecting with women from around the world, collecting stories, interviewing them for podcasts, and discovering how this abstract and altruistic idea of spirituality and motherhood can become a livelihood for us and my new life path.

I want to believe I'm living the classic entrepreneur struggle story. I walked away from my nine-to-five to pursue this mission and watched our savings quickly drain to support my new stay-at-home status.

Let's face it. Because of my health, I wouldn't have been able to go back to my job, anyway.

In the past few months, I've battled mastitis, mononucleosis, a staph infection on my face, a tailbone cyst, MRSA on my arm, a corneal cyst, second-degree burns on my fingers, extreme eczema on my hand, giant papillary conjunctivitis, tailbone bruising, and vaginal nerve damage.

I continue to assume each new thing on the above list will be the last and launch me on my true path to healing and self-enlightenment. Yet, realistically? I feel like I'm still waiting for the next shoe to drop.

I spend every day with you by my side, without much help from nearby family or friends.

Through sheer will, I've grown Enlightenedhood from an idea to a podcast with over forty conversations, an online magazine with over twenty contributing mothers, and a mission to change the consciousness of womanhood that's been viewed in over eighty countries in less than five months.

I am juggling it all. I am killin' it. I am a natural. I am Super-woman (or so I thought).

And then something happened, last week, when you were six months and four days old.

We were in California visiting Lita and Lito (your Dad's parents in case those nicknames aren't relevant by the time you read this) and I went to sleep ridiculously early because the time change fucked me up.

I awoke about an hour later to you having a complete meltdown in a nearby room.

Your teeth started to come in and your Dad was having trouble getting you to settle down.

Previous nights like this, we gave you a little bit of Tylenol to help with the pain, so I got up to find it in my suitcase and help you (and everyone else in close proximity) find relief.

See, at the time, the only way you would ingest the disgustingly sticky and grape-flavored medicine was if I shot it into the back of your mouth like a projectile missile.

Otherwise, it would slowly seep out the sides of your mouth like toxic green sludge does in the movies.

And I hate being sticky. So, I walked into the room and confidently squirted the medicine into the back of your mouth as you continued to cry.

But this time, the outcome wasn't the same.

You started choking. And then you started puking.

As your Dad screamed, "WHAT DID YOU DO?" you looked at me with such fear in your eyes as you aggressively vomited over his shoulder.

To anyone else, this probably looked like a baby crying and puking up formula at the same time, but to me, it looked like you were foaming at the mouth. It looked like you couldn't breathe.

It looked like what I had just done was going to end your life. And then I broke. And the lid of the entire volcano of lava I was trying so hard to contain...

It shattered.

It blew the lid off of my extreme loneliness and lack of in-person support.

It blew the lid off of the mourning of a body I no longer recognize that keeps betraying me.

It blew the lid off of the exhaustion of taking care of a baby for sometimes twelve hours a day, five days a week while trying to grow a business and take care of a body that still has a lot of healing to do.

It blew the lid off of feeling lost as I try to figure out how to nurture a marriage and a new child.

It blew the lid off of the crippling stress of draining finances and a quickly growing mountain of debt.

It blew the lid off unprocessed grief from losing my grandparents, friends, and relationships.

It blew the lid off of the hopelessness of your Dad's worsening back issues and inability to find a cure.

It blew the lid off of the claustrophobia of living in congested suburbia with little access to nature and green space without the overbearing energy of other people.

It blew the lid off of the fear that I stepped into a role I am not ready for or even worthy of having.

It blew the lid off of the guiltiness of dog motherhood, as I watch my polka-dotted pup's extreme anxiety resurface as my postpartum anxiety grows.

It blew the lid off of the fact that all of the above has caused me to fall into a deep and dark depression where I am completely self-aware yet don't have the time, support, or extra finances to do anything about it.

I cried for four days straight as it all started pouring out of me. Everything I thought I was strong enough to carry alone was finally too heavy.

And I don't want to carry it anymore.

The only thing I knew about postpartum before giving birth was the hospital-grade underwear women post on Instagram as badges of honor.

No one sat me down and told me how to handle the balance between extreme happiness and extreme loneliness.

No one told me that Postpartum Depression could emerge, even at six months, and look nothing like its stereotypical depiction.

No one taught me how to cope with feeling so disconnected from my body. How it wouldn't move the same, look the same or smell the same for quite some time, if ever.

No one taught me how to mourn my old body and celebrate the shit out of the miracle my new body created.

No one shared nourishing foods or supplements to help my body heal on its own time but instead made me feel ashamed when the weight on the scale wasn't going down quickly enough during each doctor's visit.

Instead, as new mothers, we are given the green light for sex and exercise at six weeks and periodically checked by an outdated and impersonal survey at our child's doctor visits to help screen for "warning signs."

As a society, mothers have six weeks to "bounce back," but the truth is, there's no turning back. Once we give birth our life is completely changed. Our bodies have completely changed. Our soul has completely changed.

Yet, somehow, we're expected to piece back together the version of us pre-pregnancy and led to feel ashamed when the puzzle pieces don't align anymore.

I'm not going to lie, I'm still learning who that new me is exactly, and it comes with a lot of questions.

Do fans of the old me even like the new me?
Do they see where I've blossomed?
Do they see me drowning?
Do they see me as just a mother now?
Do they think I'm weird when I talk about my emerging spirituality?
Do they think I'm crazy?

While I know the events of my postpartum journey may not be like yours, the emotions we as mothers go through at this time are universal.

The more women can share the truth about postpartum, the more we can set up new mothers, like you, with the support, dignity, and validation they need.

I've decided the only way to heal from my struggles is to start sharing them.

And the more I share, the more I realize that so many others feel the same.

This time has also shed light on the people in my life who aren't willing to have raw conversations about Postpartum Depression and the shadows of motherhood.

There will always be those people who will not walk alongside you as you become more vulnerable. And that's okay, too.

Being a mom is fucking hard and giving birth is one of the most traumatic things your body will ever go through.

It's also entirely beautiful. It's transcendent. It's a shared experience. And it's an amazing responsibility to guide a new soul through this crazy thing called life. I am so honored that you chose me to guide you.

One of my favorite sayings is that "When a child is born, so is a mother." So, allow me to offer advice as you go through any huge life transition, my dear: Find your village to raise you up and to help lighten the load of all you must carry.

Find a village that is willing to foster a deeper connection and willing to see you as a separate entity from your larger-than-life role as a mother.

Find a village that honors your womanhood.

And lastly, find yourself a village that will unconditionally offer support before you're ready to ask for help.

While this all may seem overwhelming, my dream is that by the time this letter becomes relevant to your own path as a mother, that the world will have changed. I know I can't stop stressing this enough.

I hope support for mothers will look a lot different and you will read all of this and say, "Duh, Mom, that's just the way things are now."

I will do everything I can to make that your reality.

With love and gratitude as deep as the universe,
Your Mama

A Letter About Boobs

Dear Luna Wilde,

When I was little, I remember looking forward to being an age where I could tuck my shirt under my boobs. All the teenagers on TV wore their t-shirts like that.

When I was twenty, I had breast reduction surgery because they had grown extremely disproportionate to my small frame.

When I was twenty-eight, nurses and lactation consultants poked, squeezed, and sighed at them as they failed to feed you during your first hours of life.

When my milk finally came in, it wouldn't come out because of the decision I made at age twenty. And while you quickly discovered my breasts would not be where your nutrients would come from without much remorse, it doesn't make the feeling of failure any easier.

I wrote you this letter not so you could forgive me, but so I could forgive myself.

I can't help but wonder if I breastfed you, would we be more in tune with one another?

If I breastfed you, would your immunity be stronger?

If I breastfed you, would I be the one you seek when you need comfort?

If I breastfed you, would I be more of a mom?

At times, I feel like I'm not a real woman or mother because my body couldn't follow through with one of the most natural processes of sustaining kin through the first months of life.

I feel so disconnected from the breastfeeding pictures I see. I feel so disconnected from one of the biggest trials and tribulations of motherhood.

And sometimes, I feel so disconnected from you.

I hope that's just the fear talking.

With love and gratitude as deep as the universe,
Your Mama

A Letter About Good Vibes

Dear Luna Wilde,

There's a misconception that spiritual people are all about "good vibes, only!" but if that were true, spirituality would be a disservice to the human experience.

When you decide to "become spiritual," it's not like your life is instantly full of rainbows, unicorns, and fucking peace signs.

To find the peace, you have to face the shadows.

Becoming a spiritual being involves looking in the mirror at the parts of yourself that you aren't proud of, and there's definitely not enough light to create a rainbow there.

I wish more people understood that making that type of commitment to yourself is a lot of hard work and a never-ending process.

Our consciousness is like an onion and we must constantly peel back layers to release wounds and traumas to be in alignment with our true selves.

Most people aren't willing to do the work and that's okay.

Perhaps they are here in this lifetime to learn or discover something different than the depths of their own heart.

We must love them just the same.

With love and gratitude as deep as the universe,
Your Mama

A Letter About Laughter

Dear Luna Wilde,

I've been learning a lot about manifesting and the Law of Attraction while you sleep.

You'll probably know it better as that thing I say, "Your thoughts create your reality," as I shake my aging finger at you like my Grandma Theresa used to do to me.

Or at least that's how I imagine it.

You see, the thing about manifesting is that it helps to match the vibrations of what you want.

So if I'm trying to attract something life-changing that is going to make me feel happier and more proud of myself than ever before, it helps to embody those feelings.

And that's where I get stuck. I can't remember the last time I felt ecstatically happy about anything. I can't remember the last time I've felt pure joy.

I've given so much of it away to others and let the shame and wounds I've been holding on to steal its glory.

Despite the lingering Postpartum Depression, I'm happy, but I don't know the me who is happy-happy, you know?

Hopefully, you don't.

P.S. I've come back to this letter to add a rebuttal. I do know what pure joy feels like. I find it in your laughter.

Don't stop laughing.

With love and gratitude as deep as the universe,
Your Mama

A Letter About Vanilla

Dear Luna Wilde,

Your Grandpa used to buy yogurt when we had tacos. He claimed it tastes the same as sour cream, but is better for you. I believe that to be true, except he always bought vanilla yogurt.

No bueno.

When your Dad makes mashed potatoes, he uses milk to add some creaminess. I believe milk is a key component to mashed potatoes, except your Dad always uses the vanilla almond milk.

Vanilla mashed potatoes. No bueno.

They say you marry men who remind you of your father.

I wonder what weird things your partner will add vanilla to.

With love and gratitude as deep as the universe,
Your Mama

A Letter About Presence

Dear Luna Wilde,

Lots of spiritual leaders these days take advantage of the idea of "finding your purpose" and it's almost ad nauseam.

What's even worse? This idea puts so much pressure on us to find that purpose and feel less than if we have no fucking clue what it means.

And then I read something today by Eckhart Tolle that changed everything.

Your purpose...is your presence.

With so many messages in our face that in order to be whole we must find this grand purpose, it's easy to feel so shitty if we don't have a "come to universe" moment about the meaning of our lives.

But what if...your only purpose at this very moment is to be present?

To read these words.

To feel your breath.

To notice the points where your body touches the Earth.

To be nothing more than just you.

Beautiful, amazing, fucking unicorn you.

Wouldn't that take a lot of the pressure off?

I'll let you sit with that for now.

With love and gratitude as deep as the universe,
Your Mama

A Letter About Bread

Dear Luna Wilde,

I didn't grow up with dogs. We had outdoor cats, carnival fish, and two cockatiels that cat called and recited the first four notes of Beethoven's Symphony No. 5.

Your Dad and I decided we wanted to adopt a dog (even though we weren't living in an apartment that allowed them) and went to the shelter to meet and greet a few.

The day I met your brother Blue, he chose me, as if he knew the exact baggage to cuddle up against. Blue's quirks prepared us well for parenthood and helped us understand the complexities of unconditional love.

I want to share a story with you, that like many of my stories, has a lesson at the end.

My favorite moment of dog motherhood is what we fondly call the "Choose Your Own Breadventure of 2015."

One thing you might remember about your dog brother is that any food left out while he was home alone became friends with his stomach very quickly.

Just a highlight reel for your enjoyment, he's eaten: A bag of four powdered cider donuts, a plate of chocolate chip cookies, an entire tub of trail mix, a bag of his own food, several bags of treats, a peanut butter and jelly sandwich, and most deliciously, trash.

One morning before work, I forgot to put my just-opened loaf of gluten-free sandwich bread back in the freezer and, sure enough, I came home to an empty bag and some crumbs.

"Fuck," I thought. "This savage forty-pound dog just ate almost an entire loaf of bread, and even more savage is the amount of money he just ate cause gluten-free bread is hella expensive."

Yes, my inner monologue has more sass and street cred in case you were wondering.

Anyway, needless to say, he went without dinner that night because he ate two-weeks of calories in one binge sesh.

Later that night, your Dad and I were sitting in bed when I felt something weird under my pillow. It was gritty and definitely foreign to the bed ecosystem.

It was a piece of bread.

At first, I was confused but then realized exactly what happened earlier that day. I jumped out of bed while hysterically laughing to follow my hunch.

I sweetly walked over to Blue, and dumped him out of his bed, flipping everything upside down.

Jackpot. Two more pieces of bread.

I walked to the front window where he spends most of his days on paw patrol and lifted up the pillow. Another piece.

Next, I made my way to the living room. There, he had placed a piece under a throw pillow and two under the couch.

Loaf complete. It was then that my view of your savage dog brother changed.

He discovered a miracle and instead of consuming it entirely in one sitting, he strategically spread it out, allowing himself to relive its gifts when he needed it most (a.k.a. when his parents never came home from work and he became an orphan who must fend for himself).

So the lesson, girl?

1. Miracles do happen. Milk the shit out of them for as long as possible.

2. Don't put all of your bread under one pillow.

With love and gratitude as deep as the universe,
Your Mama

A Letter About Views

Dear Luna Wilde,

Growing up, my family played a game in the car called "My View."

It went a little something like this:

You saw a view out the window you liked, shouted, "My view!" and the beautiful scenery became yours.

Oh, how we literally captured beauty within our own hearts.

I will teach you to do the same.

With love and gratitude as deep as the universe,
Your Mama

A Letter About Gatekeepers

Dear Luna Wilde,

I've come to a realization that has healed a lot of shame surrounding motherhood and it's this:

Mothers are the keepers of the past, present, and future.

We are the ones who have the power to stop the cycles of addiction, trauma, narcissism, unhealthy habits, broken relationships, mistrust between women, authoritative power, and so much more.

We decide that it stops with us and through going inward, have the ability to heal the generations we came from and the ones who will become our legacy.

Not only are we the cog that breaks the wheel, but we are also the greatest influencers of the next generation.

For all the times I feel alone.
For all the times I learn more about myself.
For all the times I am tested to control my reactions.

For all the times I feel failed by the system.

For all the times I heal my own body.

For all the times I create boundaries.

For all the times I follow the light and return it to others.

For all the times I need to find a few moments of peace just to survive.

They are all so I can pass these tools down to you.

So you can act through love and intention without discovering this truth after hitting rock bottom as I did.

So your amazing presence and self-empowerment will radiate to all those who know you.

I had to become a mother to help save the world.

I can't wait to save it with you.

With love and gratitude as deep as the universe,
Your Mama

A Letter About Beauty Marks

Dear Luna Wilde,

I have a lot of beauty marks on my face. Many look like constellations of the night sky. They are something I absolutely, without question, love about myself.

For the longest time, I was convinced the right person for me would be completely aware of and intoxicated by my unique yet beautiful markings.

Still to this day, not one person has ever mentioned them.

And that's okay.

We can still love parts of ourselves that others don't see.

With love and gratitude as deep as the universe,
Your Mama

A Letter About Friends

Dear Luna Wilde,

When I was in middle school, I used to decorate the ceiling of my bedroom.

One of its phases displayed neon strips of paper that listed every single one of my friends.

At night when I was in bed, I would look up in wonderment at all the beautiful people in my life.

Yet somehow, in the last twenty years, it feels like that number has gone from hundreds to zero.

I don't think there's another soul on this planet who considers me her (or his) best friend.

And that has left a huge hole in my heart.

On top of that, when I try (and try) to connect with the few I still consider dear friends, it's almost like they don't want to see me anymore.

Part of me assumes it's because I'm now a mom and they don't know how to relate to me.

Which also leaves a huge hole in my heart, because I'm still me. Now more than ever.

With love and gratitude as deep as the universe,
Your Mama

A Letter About Fog

Dear Luna Wilde,

I feel the fog finally starting to lift. I no longer feel like I'm treading through mud.

And while I still don't feel "back to normal," I do feel hopeful that the new me, the one that has rebirthed since you were conceived almost a year and a half ago, is one spectacular woman.

I wish I had a more tangible recollection of how I've made it through the past few months so I can support others who are going through the same, but to be honest, it's all a blur.

Here's what I do know:

Mothers deserve better. We deserve to have our bodies honored and celebrated. We deserve to have equal support to our babies postpartum. We deserve to have safe and compassionate spaces to discuss the struggles of this entire process.

We deserve to feel hope instead of shame.

And despite the lack of support, despite the physical and mental health battles, despite the belief I would never be whole again...

I'm still standing.

I'm still breathing...and that has created a spark.

I've always loved the saying that "A set back is only a set up for a comeback," and I'm ready.

I'm ready to heal. I'm ready to move on. I'm ready to come home.

With love and gratitude as deep as the universe,
Your Mama

A Letter About Tacos

Dear Luna Wilde,

It was your Grandma and Grandpa who gave me a very important lesson about "shoulds."

When I was in middle school, we made a life-changing decision to eat tacos for Thanksgiving Dinner. That seemingly small choice for one meal became the "Ryan Family Mexican Thanksgiving" tradition that we still celebrate twenty years later (except for the one year we tried to go back to turkey and it fucking sucked).

Not one of us likes turkey. It is a pain in the ass to cook. So why should we?

Instead, we chose Uncle Kent's famous guacamole, tacos, and tequila.

Because it made us happy. And warm and fuzzy. And prone to telling too many pirate jokes at the dinner table (and you ARRRR lucky to have missed that phase by a decade or so).

So many times, we do things we think we should. Because we're told that's the way it's always been done, but why?

My dear girl, what are you doing in your life that doesn't bring you joy? That you are doing just because you think you should?

What would life be like if you stopped doing it cold turkey?

Part of my spiritual journey has been learning that we don't always have to waste our energy on the shoulds.

You are the only one who gets to decide how to expend your power.

You are the only one who gets to decide what makes you happy.

And while I'm sure you know all of this already, it never hurts to be reminded once in a while.

With love and gratitude as deep as the universe,
Your Mama

A Letter About Unconditional Love

Dear Luna Wilde,

Not gonna lie, I think you love your Dad more than me at the moment (don't tell me if it's true).

And while my ego is wounded, I know in my heart that the unconditional love he receives from you and the way you need him more than you need me is the love he needs to heal some of his own wounds.

I am confident that you chose me to help you remember who you are and all the power that you have.

You chose your Dad to help him learn to love himself again.

What an amazing gift you are giving to both of us.

With love and gratitude as deep as the universe,
Your Mama

A Letter About Authenticity

Dear Luna Wilde,

I wish others weren't so quick to assume that I'm trying to become someone else.

I wish they understood I'm finally finding the courage to just be me.

With love and gratitude as deep as the universe,
Your Mama

A Letter About Oranges

Dear Luna Wilde,

I'd like to share one of the best fruit analogies I've ever heard. It has forever helped protect my heart from others and is brought to you today by letter orange (punny? no?).

When you squeeze an orange, what comes out? Orange juice.

So, when you squeeze (put pressure on) a human, what comes out? Whatever is on the inside.

That means that the anger, the jealousy, the malice, the fear, or whatever else is projected your way has absolutely nothing to do with you.

Knowing this might make it easier to take fewer things personally and send a lot more love to those who need it most.

With love and gratitude as deep as the universe,
Your Mama

A Letter About Christmas

Dear Luna Wilde,

It's the night before your first Christmas and you're fast asleep in your plaid-footed pajamas.

I know I should be basking in the "magic" of Christmas, but instead, I feel anxious.

Anxious that somehow you'll remember that we didn't have enough money to buy you many presents this year.

Anxious that you'll someday whole-heartedly believe that this holiday is just about extravagant gifts.

Anxious that your future behavior will be motivated by your placement on the "naughty" or "nice" list.

My parents raised me to value experiences and time with family over material items. I will do my best to plant the same seed within you.

I know as parents, Christmas is special because we get to relive the wonder through our children.

I just don't want you to believe that the only wonder in the world comes one day a year from a jolly man in a red suit who fulfills wish lists.

There's always wonder all around us.

It comes from presence.
It comes from Mother Earth.
It comes from the stars.
It comes from human connection.
It comes from love.
It comes from laughter.

It comes from moments that ignite us at our very core. And that is something that cannot be wrapped and put under a tree.

P.S. Santa isn't real and your Dad ate all of your cookies.

With love and gratitude as deep as the universe,
Your Mama

A Letter About Decades

Dear Luna Wilde,

New Year's Eve is on the top of the list of holidays I hate the most. The pressure to have an epic night that prequels the year to come often leads to major let down.

On top of that, as an empath, the anticipation that I soak up from others cripples me. As a result, I usually start bawling at midnight when it's finally released.

That's why it's 9:30 p.m., and I'm already in bed. I'm fairly certain your Dad thinks I'm extremely lame. He would never admit it to my face, but that's the thing about empaths—you don't have to say anything to our faces, we already know.

I digress. This letter is not about how lame your Dad thinks I am, but instead, what's to come in the morning.

When we wake up, it won't just be a new year or a new month, but an entirely new decade. One that I am feeling so hopeful about. One that is calling me. One that is beckoning me to thrive.

While time is a human construct, something about the idea of a clean slate in a new decade does feel revitalizing at a soul level. So, instead of resolutions, I'll share with you the woman I want to be as the 2020s begin:

I want to be a woman, who through nourishment, movement, energetic releases, and time, heals her own body from an inflamed, infection-ridden cocoon to a high-frequency vessel of light and self-love.

I want to be a woman who stops seeking the answers she thinks she wants to hear and, instead, embodies the highest version of herself.

I want to be a woman who fully understands she is already everything she ever wished to be.

I want to be a woman who stops giving her power away to what others think of her.

I want to be a woman who stops waiting for permission slips to create the life she wants.

I want to be a woman who is intentional with time and values the present moment as a gift.

And lastly, I just want to feel like a woman. Is there a switch or something that is supposed to make that happen? A certain date? Was it supposed to happen after birth? Does it happen when I get a mom haircut and a one-piece bathing suit? Hello? Is this thing on?

I still feel like a meek sixteen-year-old girl who can't legally buy a bottle of Merlot, let alone deserve the responsibility to be a mother. As I enter this new decade, I'd really like to let that girl know it's safe to move on to womanhood.

If only New Year's Eve had supernatural powers.

Bibbidi-Bobbidi-Boo! I will now be that woman as soon as the clock strikes twelve.

Oh, how I wish it was that easy, my girl. I have a lot of work ahead of me. And it will all be worth it to become that woman for you.

You deserve *that* woman as your role model.

With love and gratitude as deep as the universe,
Your Mama

A Letter About Bodies

Dear Luna Wilde,

I want nothing more than to love this new body. It led me to you. It carried me to this very moment as I write you these words.

But reprogramming the almost thirty years of conditioning that taught me that thin is beautiful? That thin is more worthy? It's no small feat.

I thought I'd share with you a love letter I wrote to my body to prove that beauty, strength, and wisdom have nothing to do with the number on the scale or pant size.

_____

To my feet, thank you for keeping me grounded as I stand tall with my connection to Mother Earth.

To my legs, thank you for carrying me through all my experiences and helping me walk the path that guided me to this very moment.

To my knees and ankles, thank you for helping me pivot and embrace change as I flow and adapt.

To my hips, thank you for your strength, support, and expansion through the life, emotions, and experiences I have carried within me.

To my womb, thank you for your miraculous gift of life and the profound ways your power has changed me.

To my navel, thank you for your nourishment, as I transitioned Earthside.

To my organs, thank you for your constant vitality and role in my self-healing capabilities.

To my heart, thank you for the love you allow me to experience in this lifetime and the unconditional space you hold for others.

To my lungs, thank you for each breath and your role in centering me with each inhale and exhale.

To my breasts, thank you for the nourishment you created for my child, despite prior surgical intervention disconnecting the pathways to be able to breastfeed. I still honor you.

To my shoulders, thank you for all the weight you carried (and continue to), and the safe space you make for others to lean on.

To my arms, thank you for allowing me to embrace others and reach towards my dreams.

To my throat and mouth, thank you for giving me my voice to create change and help heal others with my words.

To my eyes, thank you for showing me the way and allowing me to see the beauty in all things.

To my head, thank you for your endless curiosity, contemplation, and innovation.

To my body, thank you for the gifts you give me each moment.

After I wrote this letter to myself, I knew I needed to make the conscious decision to find love and acceptance in this new body.

Not just for my own confidence and worth, but so that you will never learn any patriarchy-based beauty standards from me.

True beauty comes from within. True beauty comes from the way you shine your light. True beauty comes from honoring all that you are.

Now, each time I catch myself in the mirror, I look myself straight in the eyes and say, "I love you. You are beautiful."

And that has made all the difference. Because it's true.

With love and gratitude as deep as the universe,
Your Mama

A Letter About Seasons

Dear Luna Wilde,

Now that I'm the mother of a child with teeth (did that feel as weird to read as it did to write?)—I must admit—the non-linear journey of teething surprises me.

I assumed, much like a confetti cannon, there would be a few moments of build up before an explosive pop to release the pressure. And just like that, *pop! pop! pop!* you'd have a mouth full of chompers.

Instead, there's a much less distinctive path from gums to pearly whites. One that's more beautiful than confetti. It's rather poetic if you think about it: The journey towards growth, the break though, the lull, and then, the slow ascension until a new part of you has reached its highest good.

Now that I think about it, am I really that surprised? Nah. I'm beginning to recognize the same cyclical nature in my own growth and the micro and macro seasonality of my life.

My winters and periods of darkness are just as important as the times I feel most bright and free. There's no straight line to walk, just a full trust that the ebb and flow will carry me to the same destination.

It's a natural yet foreign truth that I am attempting to honor by letting go of the expectation that this path was ever linear to begin with. As I sit here attempting to summon anything else profound I could say about the natural rhythms of life (you know I like to end my letters with lessons), this prose came to me. So I'll leave you with this instead:

For thousands of years, the flowers bloom, hoping winter will never come, as they bask in the magnificent beams of light. Yet eventually, they grow weary, constantly standing tall against the wind, the rain, and the blazing rays of the sun. They yearn for respite and surrender. When the days start to find ease and their momentum slows, the flowers let themselves go into the unknown. They trust that resurgence is part of the process of finding an inner radiance that is sovereign from and more brilliant than the sun.

With love and gratitude as deep as the universe,
Your Mama

A Letter About Eggplants

Dear Luna Wilde,

I never imagined the scenario where I'd have to calm a crying child who wasn't allowed to stick her finger up the dog's urethra.

Thanks for keeping me on my toes.

With love and gratitude as deep as the universe,
Your Mama

A Letter About Vulnerability

Dear Luna Wilde,

Vulnerability is such an underrated ingredient to a fulfilled life. These days, it is a huuuuuge buzzword thanks to my girl Brené Brown and she's right. Not only is vulnerability the new black (new book title, B.B.?), it's also magical.

I've always worn my heart on my sleeve, but being vulnerable in all aspects of my life?

It's terrifying yet fucking invigorating.

There's such a softness and grace that comes with being fully open to yourself and others (with boundaries, my girl!).

With vulnerability comes a surrender and a trust that your journey is fully supported. This act of receiving and not controlling outcomes helped me re-energize my spirit.

And now that I'm a life-long passenger on the vulnerability train, I will do everything I can to lead by example and show you the true power of vulnerability. A power that can change the world as we know it.

A world where we bravely share our experiences to help heal and empower others.

A world where we say the hard things with love.

A world where we aren't afraid to be exactly who we are.

A world where we fully trust the process of the universe.

A world where we finally see our weaknesses as our strengths.

A world where vulnerability isn't just the new black, but a mutual understanding of love, respect, and space held between humans.

See what I mean? World changing.

With love and gratitude as deep as the universe,
Your Mama

A Letter About Rain

Dear Luna Wilde,

One of my favorite things to do is to walk in the rain.

I love how everything slows down.
I love how the neighborhood becomes quiet.
I love how the rain evokes the fragrances of Mother Earth.
I love how the galvanized drops meet the warm pavement for the first time.

I love how the rain-painted air swirls around my lungs, with each inhale feeling like the release of an exhale.
I love how it grounds me.
I love how it acts like I am the only one experiencing its bliss.

I hope you will love the rain, too. It is one of my most trusted partners in self-healing.

The things that help our souls find peace and revitalization are what we need to fill up our cups, recharge, and find balance.

The things that ignite yet cleanse our very being allow us to create the space to go further inward to be fully capable of connecting with our hearts.

Even if you care more for sunny days, I hope I can help guide you to those things that ignite a remembrance of peace, light, and joy.

Still really hoping it's rain, though.

With love and gratitude as deep as the universe,
Your Mama

A Letter About Birthdays

Dear Luna Wilde,

You are one! Welcome to toddlerhood.

While you may not understand time yet in these types of milestones, I hope you can feel the love and presence from us today.

For months, I've wished for one last snowstorm to keep your Dad home with us so we can celebrate your birthday as a family.

I got my wish, but never in the way I imagined. We are currently in the midst of a pandemic. Everyone is required to stay home for the next few weeks to help lessen the wave of infected people entering the healthcare system.

When we brought you home from the hospital a year ago, I imagined I'd spend this time stressing over whether or not to throw you an over-the-top themed birthday party that seems like a rite of passage where we live.

Instead, there's a lot of collective fear and panic, uncertainty, and unnecessary battles over toilet paper. Many people are dying, everything is shut down, the economy is struggling, and we live thirty minutes away from the worst of it in New York City.

While that sounds scary, we have everything we could ever need, and I am so grateful for this time to watch you grow, safe at home.

This morning, your Dad finally gave in and let us watch *Frozen 2*. I don't know if it is the fact I now have a one year old, or that Elsa's self-awakening is so deeply similar to my own, but I bawled through the entire movie.

After your nap, we plopped you in your high chair and set up a live stream for friends and family to sing "Happy Birthday" and watch you have no interest in the strawberry iced cupcake your Dad braved the virus to pick up for you at the store.

I believe you will walk any day now. Once you are freed by your own steps, I know the world will become grander for your eager soul.

As you continue to grow, I pray you will never know this time of global crisis. No matter how long this lasts, I will keep our little bubble safe and healthy at all costs.

And if you remember anything about this time, I hope it's how society bent the rules so we could bond as a family unit, find gratitude and presence, and celebrate life. Especially yours.

Happy birthday, my moon girl. Here's to many more.

With love and gratitude as deep as the universe,
Your Mama

A Letter About Vagabonds

Dear Luna Wilde,

There's still very much a part of me that identifies as a vagabond.

Without the constant effort to trust and ground, I find it easy to embody a helium balloon, slowly drifting into the unknown as I deflate.

I've lived ten places in the last ten years and the exhaustion is starting to catch up to me.

I no longer want to be the girl who, at twenty one, got a tattoo of a feather behind her ear because that's what she thought she'd always be...an after-thought of the flock, floating away as her origins disappeared into the sky.

Instead, I want to return to the way of my ancestors and honor the space Mother Earth provides to build our home, lay my head, raise my family, and harvest the food that's generously at my table.

I want roots.

I want a true place to call home.

Beyond the pride of a space that is uniquely ours, I believe it's a necessary part of our growth.

Why? Because if our basic needs of shelter and safety are not met, we are not able to fully ground.

Without this solid foundation, we will never feel secure enough to go beyond our human experience. And isn't that what I've been trying to share with you all along?

That there are infinite possibilities to find if we can look beyond our human constructs?

I hope we will have the means to discover that place soon.

Literally and figuratively.

With love and gratitude as deep as the universe,
Your Mama

A Letter About Dichotomies

Dear Luna Wilde,

I've always thought of myself as a walking dichotomy: An extroverted introvert who yearns to be wild and free yet feels most secure as a homebody.

Welp, it seems my contradictions got the best of me…again.

For months, I've felt the pressure building. It's as if I'm on the inside of a balloon about to burst, ready to reveal the new and improved, spiritual as fuck version of me.

But that point of resistance I feel so deeply? It isn't physics or waiting for a grand permission slip from the universe. It is a physical wall of fear built by yours truly.

I wanted to evolve so quickly that I overlooked the very process of transformation I am so preachy about in these letters: To move forward, I have to heal what's holding me back.

Fear is holding me back.

Fear is holding me back? Wow. That feels cathartic yet devastating to write.

I'm straddled between versions of myself. What if the new me can't simultaneously exist in the same relationships as the old? What if the people in my life don't like or understand the new? What if I'm no longer enough for them to stay?

Will this quest to find my true self be worth it if I end up completely alone and unloved? Is my own wholeness worth the risk?

Annnnd cue the internal battle of the human's dichotomy between the highest self and the ego. One endlessly nudges us towards growth and the other consistently reminds us that change is dangerous.

I wish I could end this letter by telling you the basic instinct to resist change is easy to overcome.

I wish I could tell you that growth is as easy as identifying self-created barriers and TNT'ing the shit out of them.

Boom! Everything standing in your way is now dust. Not.

I wish I could tell you that karmic wounds such as abandonment and unworthiness can be released in one round of introspection. Oftentimes, they have many layers.

The hope I *can* leave with you, my girl? Let me try to bring this full circle.

Sometimes physics *is* the answer (well, kind of—stay with me). Newton's Third Law of Motion formally states that for every action there is an equal and opposite reaction.

That means for all the love you wish to receive, you must start by giving love, especially to yourself.

The more you love yourself, whole-heartedly, in each new version, the more the universe will reciprocate that love in return.

Sometimes love is all we have, but it *is* enough. And that, my dear, seems worth the risk.

With love and gratitude as deep as the universe,
Your Mama

A Letter About American Pie

Dear Luna Wilde,

I can remember the first moment I fell in love with photography. I took a picture of your Aunt Chloe jumping off Grandma and Grandpa's porch.

Back in those days, we didn't get instant access to our pictures. I needed a chaperone to bring the film to Eckerd's, hand over my allowance, wait a week for it to develop, and then hope and pray that there would be a few winning prints inside a mysterious white paper envelope.

That picture of your Aunt Chloe? It was a masterpiece. I captured her suspended in mid-air. Within that picture, I became captivated by the profoundness of photography's ability to press pause on each moment with such beauty.

When I was in high school and digital photography became more accessible, I started to hone my craft. Everyone knew me as the girl who took pictures and it helped heal part of the wounds of the girl who used to be known for sports and music.

Photography felt like my calling. It was such an effortless form of self-expression and taking pictures made me start to feel whole again. It came naturally to me because I always saw the world through a photographer's lens (still do).

During my junior year, my work was submitted to an art show at Ithaca College. The purpose was for us high schoolers to receive feedback from faculty to help prepare for a college portfolio and curriculum.

I can remember waiting as the professors waded through aisles of matted work towards me, excited and hopeful to know what they thought of my photographs.

When a woman finally approached me, she said nothing.

She stared for what felt like hours. When she finally opened her mouth, she shared that she was completely under-whelmed and that my pictures, my pride and joy, the mani-festations of my self-worth, did absolutely nothing for her.

And that one moment of defeat is a primary anchor of my "not good enough" story.

On that day, I decided the way I saw the world was not worthy and definitely not beautiful.

I decided that my creative expression was mediocre at best.

And I declared that the outwardly creative version of me was not seen by the rest of the world like it was in my own delusional reality.

And that is when my self-expression started to wither away. It was a slow death as my creativity disconnected from my soul, inch by inch.

Now, as I sit here almost fifteen years later, trying to heal the emotional baggage I've refused to acknowledge, I had an epiphany.

As I dig towards the root of my relationships wound, I was determined to find the person who was the cause of my seemingly countless failed friendships and romantic partners.

And then it hit me like a tidal wave while I was in the shower. It was a soft voice that said, "You let the music die."

And then I saw it all in reverse. The heartache. The abandonment. But the one who started it all?

It was me.

I failed to honor my relationship with my creative self and I
let others take the blame for it.

Because I let a part of myself go, I made it a precedent in
relationships to never allow myself to be fully honored. To
never be fully seen.

I'm sharing this with you for a few reasons (yes, another lesson at the end, shocker!).

First, it's easier to believe that others are at fault for our
wounds. As a result, instead of taking responsibility for the
ways we've fallen out of alignment with our true self, we
assume the capability to heal them lies externally.

Forgiveness is one of the greatest gifts we can give ourselves. Celebrate your ability to recognize your missteps. It
makes the journey towards your highest self feel like much
more of a homecoming.

Second, never compare your self-expression to anyone else. The self is included because it's a practice that is unique to you and to you only.

The world will be full of labels, competitions, and others who will try to make you feel unworthy because that's how they secretly feel on the inside. Your opinion is the only one that matters. Your creative expression is such a beautiful Divine Feminine gift we are given in this human experience.

Please don't let there come a day where you discover the art, the music, or whatever it is that lights you up has died.

With love and gratitude as deep as the universe,
Your Mama

A Letter About Effort

Dear Luna Wilde,

For most of my life, I've been able to coast as a high-achiever while only exerting about 65% of my effort.

Oftentimes, I do wonder if my life would have turned out differently if I put my full effort into things like athletics, music, filmmaking, or art, but I also know that's not the way it was supposed to happen.

As I write this, to the outside world, it looks like we are failing. We have no money and I have no "job." But the truth? I've never felt more alive or free. This self-healing and self-discovery journey I am on has been the first thing, I think in my entire life, that I've given 100%.

And that pride? That power? That self-acceptance that comes with this work? That is something that no amount of money can buy. And to me, that makes me rich.

With love and gratitude as deep as the universe,
Your Mama

A Letter About Oz

Dear Luna Wilde,

The Wizard of Oz is braided into my psyche. You can thank your Grandpa for that.

Up until recently, I identified with Dorothy. Looking for life beyond the rainbow on a never-ending quest to find a mysterious wizard who would sew up my wounds and help me find home.

As my life continues to come full circle while I heal, I want to share a letter I wrote to myself in 2010 as a junior in college:

> *Hey, you.*
>
> *I'm tired. I haven't stopped moving for three years. This school. That school. Some place. This friend. That boy. I have no establishments. No roots. No foundation. I'm on the run, looking for signs.*
>
> *I'm young. I'm impressionable. I am Dorothy, expecting the journey to my destiny to be a simple stroll*

down a masoned path. As a child, I never realized that the Yellow Brick Road would have tolls, diversions, conflict. I was naïve to assume what was on the other side of the rainbow.

Life used to be all about performing. I was addicted to the thrill, to the euphoria. I had the biggest thirst to be someone, and leave my mark on this world. I played the parts, sang the songs, and danced in the twinkling spotlights. I was the show and life was the stage. I had passions, dreams, and talents. The lime-light was beaten out of my soul, in one strike. One strike was all it took.

The first time I was hit across the face, I was doing his homework. A jack-of-all-trades, me the artist, fill-ing in his lack of creativity. Filling in his ignorance. The poster I was making was already planned out. The lines already drawn, and all space accounted for. I was going to retrace my steps, enhance the graphite lines with ruby red glitter. It was going to be a mas-terpiece.

All I had to do was follow the narrow stick nodes.

But, my elbow's footing slipped, and I stepped off my path.

And he struck me. He broke my confidence, my consciousness.

After that day, I collapsed into a field of poppies.

Foggy. Hazy. Diffident of my way.

Like most, I always dreamed of high school being comparable to the movies: Laughter, friends, and midnight kisses.

Not tears, solitude and late-night calls that he's cheated, again. Follow the...just watch your step so he doesn't hit you again.

He threatened I'm nothing, and I used to believe it. I'm nothing, I'm nobody, maybe I don't exist. I don't exist.

Years later, now at my third college in three years, sometimes I still wonder, do I exist? I don't exist. No one knows my name. They don't know me, I don't know me.

But, they will. And I'm going to know me, too, so I'm off to see The Wizard.

I seek courage. Strength to accept my flaws and bravery to push my own limits. Courage to follow my heart, and to trust nothing less. I've been so afraid of falling that I forgot that you must fall to soar. I want the courage to build myself back up, to assemble towards the sky, and not stop until I reach the stars.

I seek a brain. I will forever seek knowledge. I thrive on knowledge. I'm quenched by being intellectual and I'm comforted by the thought of rising above ignorance. I want to be cultured, unbiased, enlightened and cultivated.

I seek a heart. To love with reckless abandon. My heart is open to endless adorations and has a resounding light that has the power to heal and the power to forgive. My heart will have infinite space yet will always be full. I seek a heart that can look past insecurities. That can look past flaws. A heart made of diamonds, unbreakable by mankind.

I seek a place to call home. To find what anchors me. A solid foundation, and a place of definition. I want roots, I want growth, and I will blossom. I'll have a storm cellar, able to withstand tempestuous storms.

There's no place like home. I'm ready to come home.

Ten years since writing this letter, I have everything I set out to find. I wish I could let that lost girl know that just a decade later, she will return home from Oz. Perhaps she innately knew.

The only thing I didn't expect? That it would be me, instead of The Wizard, on the other side of that curtain.

Never forget that everything you seek is already within you, my dear girl. You have all of the answers. Even if it takes you longer than expected to find it.

Follow the Yellow Brick Road and trust that, even if it departs from the beaten path, it will always lead you home.

With love and gratitude as deep as the universe,
Your Mama

A Letter About Camps

Dear Luna Wilde,

Just when I assumed motherhood is one big club, I quickly discovered I was wrong. I feel forced to choose a camp, much like a Hogwarts house, and defend it at all costs.

Will I fight for 'Breast is best?' Anti-vax? Cry it out? Home-schooling? Working moms? All-natural moms? The list goes on and on and frankly, it's exhausting (and isolating).

Why does motherhood have to be another form of divisive-ness? Shouldn't we support each other on this journey with the mutual understanding that the only true camp is the one where we all show up to be the best us and the best leader for our children?

Where is that camp, huh? My Hufflepuff friends and I want to join.

With love and gratitude as deep as the universe,
Your Mama

A Letter About Validation

Dear Luna Wilde,

Women in my generation were raised to give so much of our power away. We were taught to be quiet, to seek outside validation from others, systems, and authority figures, and float with the current because it's always been done that way.

As a result, we're still waiting for permission slips, giving our power away to what others think of us, and on a constant quest for answers from outside sources.

My latest "aha!" moment came when I realized I have all the answers. I have all the power to make my own decisions, be my own person, and create a life that is completely intentional and self-designed.

But believing it? That's still a work in progress. Here are just a few times I stood in my own way recently:

1. Constantly questioning my intuition and letting my ego attribute Divine guidance to my imagination.

2. Weakening the energetic vibrations of my body through indulgence in man-made (lab-made) "food."

3. Consuming social media and video content that I thought was more enriching than silent and present time within my own heart.

4. Assuming there is a checklist I must complete to climb up the spiritual ladder and become "enlightened."

5. Comparing myself to other women's spiritual and motherhood journey.

6. Uniting my body size and postpartum healing with my self-worth.

7. Allowing perceived judgment of my spirituality stop me from authentically showing up.

8. Allowing other women's (again, perceived) opinions of me dictate what I believe to be true about myself.

9. Assuming the answers to who I really am exist outside of myself.

10. Thinking there was ever anything standing in my way to begin with.

In case it didn't sink in the first time, let me repeat:

There is absolutely nothing standing in your way.

Trust that you have the compass, the answers, and the personal power to declare that whoever you wish to be is beautiful, worthy, whole, and absolutely enough.

The only validation you need for all of the above to be true is your own.

With love and gratitude as deep as the universe,
Your Mama

A Letter About Bananas

Dear Luna Wilde,

Today, you slipped in your own pee on the kitchen floor.

It was as if you literally slipped on a banana peel.

Thanks for the laugh.

With love and gratitude as deep as the universe,
Your Mama

A Letter About Pandemics

Dear Luna Wilde,

In case you were wondering, we're still home, sheltering in place, to stop the spread of COVID-19. So much for two weeks. It's been over four months.

After I made the decision to choose gratitude over fear, this time locked away at home is such a blessing.

We've watched you grow into a toddler, the seasons change from winter to spring to summer, and the biggest transformation of all?

Me. I've transitioned from caterpillar to goop to butterfly.

And now I'm ready to soar. (Six feet away from everyone else, of course.)

With love and gratitude as deep as the universe,
Your Mama

A Letter About the Patriarchy

Dear Luna Wilde,

I never thought I'd become a feminist, but as I look deeper into my own shadows and the root of my wounds, all I have to say is...

Fuck the patriarchy.

With love and gratitude as deep as the universe,
Your Mama

A Letter About Blood

Dear Luna Wilde,

I recently started using menstrual cups as a way to be more sustainable while honoring my cycle.

The first time I removed it from my body, I was expecting to be disgusted by the grotesque sheddings of my uterus.

But the truth?

What resided in my menstrual cup was the most beautiful thing I have ever seen.

The blood shimmered in a way I can only describe as divine. It was pure. It was celestial. It was like seeing a glimpse of God.

My generation was raised to see our monthly blood as gross, dirty, and something that ignited shame.

I started bleeding when I was just eleven years old.

I felt so confused and ashamed that I hid my stained under-wear in the back of my closet until my Mom found it months later. She was so hurt I didn't come to her, but how could I?

I was never taught it was beautiful. I was never taught it was part of my ancient power. I was never taught about its cycli-cal partnership with Mother Earth and Grandmother Moon.

Instead, I was taught by our society that my blood should be hidden. I was taught it is the scapegoat for my emotional outbursts and actions that go beyond the monotonous. I was taught it is an inconvenience to modern-day womanhood.

Yet, what I've discovered as I step into owning my woman-hood, is that this blood is sacred. This blood continues to shed old versions of me. This blood carries my DNA that we now share.

This blood, without fail, continues a cycle of death and rebirth within my womb that connected me to you.

With love and gratitude as deep as the universe,
Your Mama

A Letter About Spiritual Gifts

Dear Luna Wilde,

Good news, I'm fully out of the spiritual closet. Although, not really, because so much of what I continue to learn about my soul is done quietly and privately. The difference is, I now feel comfortable showing up as my whole self.

So much of my quest to discover my spiritual gifts was driven by my ego, probably to feel special and different.

See there it is, again. Needy for outside validation much?

While I was cooped up in the closet like Harry Potter under the stairs, I thought finding my spiritual gifts would give me the confidence I needed to burst down the door.

That's where I was wrong. I was never separated from them in the first place.

I thought acknowledging my spiritual gifts as a claircognizant star being and Atlantean High Priestess who can influence human energy fields and weather patterns, connect to the other side, and channel Mary Magdalene and other Ascended Masters would be a gift to my identity, but I'm humbled by the truth.

The most profound spiritual gift I have received? Love.

I believed my greatest love story would be with someone else. Cue the fairytale ending as my soulmate and I walk off into the proverbial sunset.

The love story I never expected? One with just me.

It's as if my heart was set on fire. The love I continue to culti-vate for myself is one of my life's greatest blessings.

And now, I am able to radiate even more love to you, as if that was even possible.

With love and gratitude as deep as the universe,
Your Mama

A Letter About Autopilot

Dear Luna Wilde,

As I get in further into this whole "being an adult" thing, I've discovered something earth-shattering.

My parents are just humans.

One day you, too, will realize I am a mere muggle. So, I'd like to come clean.

I've done a lot of things I am not proud to admit. I've hurt people. Never intentionally, but because I couldn't act beyond the demons of my own wounds.

After I transferred schools before my sophomore year of college, I was lost and lived the next four years without a conscious being in the driver's seat.

I indulged in fast food, drugs, alcohol, manipulation, lies, and got lost in the identity as the mysterious broken girl.

I truly believed that I could get away with whatever I wanted.

And I did.

But it was not a role I could play for too long, because self-destruction and causing harm to others are not aligned with my best self.

When I finally turned off the autopilot, the guilt and the shame caught up with me. I've since been figuring out how to let go of the wounds that caused me to act out of alignment and forgive the version of myself that took on the world with empty intention.

To me, that's what being human is all about.

To evolve, we must be loving enough to identify our mistakes with grace, humility, and forgiveness. We must be brave enough to admit when we are wrong. We must be willing enough to take the necessary steps toward growth.

I promise to be loving, brave, and willing to evolve for you.

With love and gratitude as deep as the universe,
Your Mama

A Letter About Privilege

Dear Luna Wilde,

As I continue to step into my truth as a spiritual teacher, I'm frustrated by the way capitalism has clouded the true intention of a spiritual practice.

There should not be privilege in spirituality, otherwise, it is just another form of oppression and another form of divisiveness.

If we continue to depict spirituality as a skinny white woman's "self-care" then we are missing the point.

Spirituality isn't about meditating on beaches, crystal collections, access to the best healers or psychics, or prancing in a wildflower field like an ethereal goddess.

Yes, all of those things can prove valuable to a spiritual journey (I, myself, like to prance in fields), but there needs to be an end to this sparkly FOMO culture that "spiritual influencers" have created to prey on soul searchers.

142

Otherwise, a journey that is unique, sacred, and available to every human on this planet becomes inaccessible without certain prerequisites.

And that is something, my dear girl, that does not sit right with me.

Here's the real truth about spirituality that I discovered through my own self-development and conversations with hundreds of spiritual women from around the world:

1. Spirituality is called a practice because it is a consistent effort towards growth and soul-discovery. It's never perfect and usually feels like you're doing it wrong. But that's the point.

2. You don't need to buy anything to be spiritual. Yes, tools like crystals, tarot cards, and smudge sticks can enhance your practice, but they are objects that are infused with your power and your intention. Not the other way around.

3. You don't need to attend a retreat or go on a spiritual sabbatical to become enlightened. Yes, I know this kind of experience is on many of our bucket lists, but moms

especially may not have time and resources available. And that's okay. It doesn't make you any less spiritual.

4. Spirituality isn't just about the sparkly or the Instagram-worthy images. True transformation is messy, ugly, and uncomfortable as fuck. Oftentimes, it happens in the midst of the chaos, and when you least expect it.

5. No one can do the hard work for you. That is up to you and you alone. Yes, find the mentors who can be your accountability partner and your guide. Spiritual teachers, who operate with integrity, will lead you to discover the answers yourself and remind you there is no fast-pass to soul growth.

6. Spirituality transcends religion, economic status, race, gender, and culture. It is not "New Age" or "woo woo," but an ancient practice of coming home to yourself. A practice that helps you grow from your tribulations and lead with intention, gratitude, and, most importantly, love.

7. Spirituality is not about ego, but oneness. You are more than your unique human experience. You are an interconnected light-filled being woven into the fabric of the universe.

8. A healthy spiritual practice doesn't mean you have to become a spiritual entrepreneur. We need grounded and conscious beings who work in our healthcare, technology, government, education systems, and other capitalistic structures, too.

9. The idea of "finding your purpose" or needing to describe your spiritual gifts with labels are man-created constructs. Our connection to the energy of the universe, in whatever personal modality that looks like, extend beyond your human experience.

10. Your life experiences are intentionally placed before you for growth. Your spiritual practice allows you to see these moments as opportunities for expansion and honor the unexpected path of life. Always trust that your journey is not only sacred but co-created with your best intentions in mind.

Just like many of these letters I write to you, it is my hope that by the time you read this, these words will be truths you already know.

I hope that spirituality will no longer be stigmatized, but instead, a sacred inner voice that always guides us home to our innate truth of unity, compassion, sovereignty, gratitude, and love.

I hope the highest good of a spiritual practice will overcome the greed and privilege that proliferate where spirituality intersects with capitalism.

I hope that each woman awakens to her power, divine connection to the universe, and realizes that she is in fact, her own guru.

I hope that spirituality will be a privilege, not because of skin color or net worth, but because being human is the only requirement.

I know your generation will help make all of these things true. You will be the ones to bring spirituality back home to the heart space of each and every soul.

And that simple yet profound act will change the world as we know it.

With love and gratitude as deep as the universe,
Your Mama

A Letter About Age

Dear Luna Wilde,

Today, I am (finally) thirty years old.

It feels strange to admit this outside of my own mind, but I feel like I'm of the age where people might start taking me serious-

...shit. There it is again.

It's funny how my need for external validation continues to pop up where I least expect it. I thought this letter would be a victory anthem for my thirties but let me unpack this instead (maybe there's a lesson here, who knows).

I can't remember a time when I didn't want to be older. I've always had older friends and tend to feel out of place with people my own age.

On top of that, because of my youthful face, people assume I'm much younger than I actually am. They are usually a good ten years off. (Yes, Karen. I know it will be a "good thing" when I'm older. Whatever that means.)

As a result, I've spent my entire life trying to prove that I'm not only my biological age but my wise soul age, too. It's exhausting.

I thought when I made it to thirty, my birthday would include a rite of passage through a sparkly tunnel into the land of "Mad Respect and Presumed Badass-ery."

Yes, that's its official name.

But there is no tunnel and there is no green light to feeling worthy and confident. Those are qualities I need to evoke within myself.

I guess there is a lesson here, girl, but for me. Let's try this over again:

Today, I am thirty years old and I am ready for people to start taking me seriously.

With love and gratitude as deep as the universe,
Your Mama

A Letter About Lineage

Dear Luna Wilde,

Did you know a woman carries her grandchildren in her womb for five months of her pregnancy? It's one of the many ways we, as women, are inextricably connected through our lineage.

You come from a succession of feisty and independent women. It's energy that's within you, too.

When our existences blend together like layers of a water-color painting, our lineage becomes a superhighway for ancestral baggage.

It's easy to recognize passed-down characteristics like resilience, intellect, and dainty wrists, but much harder to identify the energetic thorns we unconsciously carry generation after generation.

Over two years ago, I wrote you a letter after my mother's mother died. Her passing opened my eyes to the role I can play in our line of women. I promised you I'd let go of all that does not serve me so my emotional baggage does not define you. I have worked every day since to keep it.

The weight of this responsibility grows as I go further within my own heart, so I'd like to add to my promise:

I promise to embody the Divine Mother to access my self-healing capabilities and break the cycle of any ancestral energy that no longer serves our lineage, takes away our power, or keeps us from the light.

I promise to pass down to you spiritual truths about womanhood, motherhood, ascension, the Earth, the Moon, the Cosmos and beyond, returning to the ways of our lineage before this information was lost.

Lastly, I promise to help you recognize whether or not what you're experiencing is yours or something that accidentally made it through the roadblocks I set up on our ancestral highway.

Karma always finds its way, but don't worry, we'll be ready.

With love and gratitude as deep as the universe,
Your Mama

A Letter About Ego

Dear Luna Wilde,

I have to admit—when I stepped into my highest self, I assumed there would be fireworks.

I imagined my whole spirit team would gather with the archangels and other super important higher-dimensional beings and throw me a kick-ass homecoming/remembering party.

Instead, it humbled me. Union with my highest self blessed me with a soft, yet all-knowing power that is without ego.

I am completely consumed by the weight of love in my heart space and the actualization that I am infinite.

Never forget the infinite cosmos exists within you and not the other way around.

With love and gratitude as deep as the universe,
Your Mama

A Letter About Light

Dear Luna Wilde,

I am cracked wide-open but in the most radiant way possible. There is endless light pouring out of me and I know deep in my soul I am meant to share it with the world.

The only way I can describe this sensation is...it's as if my heart is directly anchored to the Divine.

The same vision keeps appearing in my meditations and my dreams. I'm standing on the edge of a cliff, surrounded by others like me who sparkle in the sunlight (not too different from Edward Cullen in *Twilight*, but I'm def not a vampire in this vision). Across a deep canyon, there is a large group of people, running from a cloud of darkness that has cornered them at the edge. Those of us standing in the light on the other side create a bridge, allowing those fleeing to step into a new world and into safety.

So what does it mean, exactly? My interpretation is that there will soon be a mass exodus from the current paradigm (i.e. oppressive patriarchy-based systems and group-think) into the light (i.e. love, equality, and unity). Through my own heart, I will be able to guide and help others. It's a mission I've slowly, and seemingly unconsciously, prepared for as I write you these letters.

By the time you read this, we may already be there. And like I've said before, I imagine you will laugh and think to yourself, "Duh, Mom. That's just the way things are."

As a mother, I can only hope that is the world you know.

I'm sure you can tell by now that I'm different. I'm not the same wounded girl that started writing to you when she thought no one else would listen.

And while you are still my most-trusted confidant, I must admit, as I step into this new version of me, I no longer feel the need to dwell on the past or explain my wounds.

They are a part of my story but no longer a part of me.

I am free. I am the light. And so are you.

With love and gratitude as deep as the universe,
Your Mama

A Letter About Hearts

Dear Luna Wilde,

And just like that, you're not only walking but running.

As I continue to marvel in how fast you've grown, I can't help but be mesmerized by the way your body leads with its heart space.

Your light and your heart arrive first before your toddler body catches up. It is quite a sight to see.

And I know this isn't a coincidence. You have a heart the world has been waiting on for centuries.

With love and gratitude as deep as the universe,
Your Mama

A Letter About Hope

Dear Luna Wilde,

I hope you think I'm brave.
I hope you think I'm weird (in a good way).
I hope you know how hard I am working to create a new
world for you.

One that you knew would be different.
One that beckoned you to this lifetime on Earth.
One that led you to choose me as your Mom.

The world is all the better because you chose me.

Thank you, thank you, thank you.

With love and gratitude as deep as the universe,
Your Mama

A Letter About You

Dear You,

The words I'm about to share with you transcend space and time. They are the reason your eyes have found this page and the closing message I wish to leave with you:

Just as the flower takes its time to unbind, the wild feather gently kisses the air, or the Earth softly spins to reveal the light, you are slowly yet remarkably awakening to your highest good.

It will not be until you catch a glimpse of yourself in a physical or metaphorical mirror when you will finally see...you are different. You have grown. You are You. You are home.

But until that moment? Keep following the nudges to blossom, honor the slight pivots in your path, and always keep the light within your heart. The best is yet to come.

With love and gratitude as deep as the universe,
Leena

A Letter About Capitalization

Dear Grammar Police,

Like you, I am strict about grammar. So, I get it. You may have cringed every time you noticed the word *universe* go uncapitalized (83 times to be exact). Please know, this was completely intentional. I apologize for any pain it may have caused you. Here's the logic behind my decision:

The Universe is a scientifically-discovered, measurable, and (mostly) tangible place agreed upon by humans.

Yet, the intangible? The existence that goes beyond our human comprehension? The things we know, but cannot see? That is the universe.

And I couldn't write a book about soul discovery without acknowledging there is so much more than we can "see."

With love and gratitude as deep as the (uncapitalized) universe,
Leena

Acknowledgments

To my husband, Stephen. Thank you for your endless support and trust in me. I am in awe of how you love our moon girl. Thank you for giving me the space to find myself and follow my dreams. What a beautiful life we have.

To my parents, Lisa and Bruce. Thank you for raising me to follow my heart and never pressuring me to become anything but myself. I am so grateful for your willingness to listen and support.

To my sister, Chloe. Thank you for picking me up when I fall, honoring our differences, and being not just a sister, but a life-long companion with a heart of gold.

To my in-laws, Angela and Rafael. Thank you for your unwavering support. I am so grateful for your continuous love and how important family is to you.

To my grandparents, Gerald and Theresa. Thank you for guiding me from the other side. I am so grateful for the connection we now share.

To my star sister, Jenny. Thank you for being the light that continues to walk with me towards my highest truth. I am so grateful to have someone who sees me for all that I am.

To my first (fuzzy) child, Blue Maracuya. Thank you for teaching me about unconditional love and patience. You're my boy, Blue.

To my dear friend, Katie. Thank you for being the first to show me that as mothers, we don't have to carry any identity other than our own or take ourselves too seriously.

To my soul family at House of Enlightenedhood. Thank you for your sisterhood, your unconditional love, your support, and your acknowledgement that mothers are so goddamn powerful.

About the Author

As a leading millennial voice in spirituality, Leena Lemos is on a mission to co-create a new paradigm of spirituality fueled heart through community and spiritual wisdom that returns to the roots of our existence.

Leena channels higher realms through the heart-space of the universe. Through this connection, Leena offers healing and guidance helping others remember the Divine light within. Leena is an inspirational speaker, wisdom keeper, and host of the House of Enlightenedhood podcast. Her having-coffee-with-a-friend approach to spirituality empowers listeners to honor the sacred dance between the spiritual and human experience. To connect with Leena or learn more about her work, visit www.LeenaLemos.com.

Find Leena on Instagram @IAmLeenaLemos.

More About House of Enlightenedhood™

House of Enlightenedhood is a spiritual cooperative, uniting in the frequency of love to build the New Earth through supportive containers for spiritual healing, growth and expansion.

To learn more about House of Enlightenedhood or to join its spiritual village and sacred online gathering space, visit www.HouseofEnlightenedhood.com.

Follow on Instagram @Enlightenedhood.

Made in the USA
Las Vegas, NV
04 December 2021

36075192R00104